BLIZZARDS:
CAUSES AND EFFECTS

by Liam Corrigan

STORY LIBRARY
MORE TO EXPLORE

www.12StoryLibrary.com

12-Story Library is an imprint of Bookstaves.

Developed and produced for 12-Story Library by Focus Strategic Communications Inc.

Library of Congress Cataloging-in-Publication Data
Name: Corrigan, Liam (Author of juvenile literature), author.
Title: Blizzards : causes and effects / by Liam Corrigan.
Description: Mankato, Minnesota : 12-Story Library, [2022] | Series: Wild weather |
Includes bibliographical references and index. | Audience: Ages 10–13 | Audience: Grades 4–6
Identifiers: LCCN 2020017442 (print) | LCCN 2020017443 (ebook) | ISBN 9781645821458
(library binding) | ISBN 9781645821830 (paperback) | ISBN 9781645822189 (pdf)
Subjects: LCSH: Blizzards—Juvenile literature.
Classification: LCC QC926.37 .C65 2022 (print) | LCC QC926.37 (ebook) | DDC 551.55/5—dc23
LC record available at https://lccn.loc.gov/2020017442
LC ebook record available at https://lccn.loc.gov/2020017443

About the Cover

A snow plow clears snow during a blizzard.

Access free, up-to-date content on this topic plus a full digital version of this book. Scan the QR code on page 31 or use your school's login at 12StoryLibrary.com.

Table of Contents

Not Just a Snowstorm

Blizzards may look pretty, but are still dangerous.

Blinding snow tumbles down. It is a severe snowstorm called a blizzard.

The National Weather Service (NWS) defines a blizzard as a storm in which winds gust at over 35 miles per hour (56 km/h). Blowing snow reduces visibility to less than one quarter of a mile (0.4 km). The storm must also last three hours or more. All of these conditions must be met to be a blizzard.

All winter storms are dangerous. Blizzards can be deadly for people and animals caught unprepared. Spending time outside in a blizzard is risky. Gusting winds and frigid temperatures create windchill. Windchill measures how cold the air feels on the skin. It increases the risk of frostbite and hypothermia. Hypothermia, or low body heat, can cause death.

Pets and farm animals should stay inside during a blizzard.

Heavy snow and strong winds can knock down power lines and trees. Power outages and frozen water pipes cause problems. Driving can be deadly due to whiteouts.

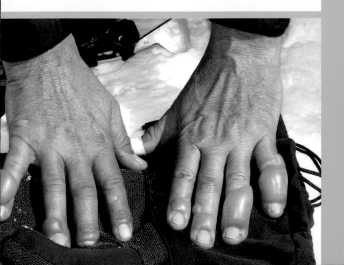

-40°

Temperature in degrees Fahrenheit (−40°C) at which frostbite can occur in less than 10 minutes

- Blizzard winds can make 20° Fahrenheit (−7°C) temperatures feel below 0° Fahrenheit (−18°C).
- Frostbite occurs when skin cells freeze. Blisters form when the skin warms up.
- The word *blizzard* used to mean *the sound of many rifles firing*.

2

A Blizzard When It's Not Snowing

Wind can make it hard to see.

Imagine playing outside in fresh snow. Suddenly, the wind blows hard. The snow swirls. That may be the beginning of a ground blizzard.

A ground blizzard may happen when cold air rushes to a snowy area. The temperature drops very quickly, and the wind gusts. A ground blizzard features strong winds, blowing snow, and cold temperatures just like a "normal" blizzard. The difference is that new snow might not fall.

78

Amount of snow in inches (198 cm) dumped in 24 hours on an Alaskan camp station in 1963

- Ground blizzards are common in Antarctica.
- During a ground blizzard, the sky can be clear and sunny.
- The winds and cold temperatures can quickly freeze your skin.

Ground blizzards tend to happen in wide open spaces. If there are trees or tall buildings, the wind can't blow the snow as far. So ground blizzards are more common on the open prairies than in urban areas or forests.

A ground blizzard can cause whiteouts. It is very dangerous to drive. People can get lost walking.

THE CHILDREN'S BLIZZARD

In January 1888, a fierce blizzard burst across the Northwest Plains in the US. No one knew the storm was coming. The wind and snow swallowed children walking home from school. The blizzard caused 235 deaths.

The Makings of a Blizzard

The Rocky Mountains seen from space.

The landscape of the US actually attracts blizzard conditions. In the West, the Rocky Mountains form a giant wall. They extend from Alaska to Mexico. These giant peaks funnel cold air south from Canada.

Meanwhile, vast grassy plains draw warm, wet air north from the Gulf of Mexico. The two air masses swirl together. The lighter hot air jumps over the cold air. Clouds form. Rain falls and forms snow. Meanwhile, the spiraling air masses create fast winds. A blizzard is born.

On the East Coast, cold air can come from the Arctic around Hudson Bay or from the Atlantic Ocean. This frigid

air collides with warm moist air from the Gulf of Mexico. It may lead to an East Coast blizzard.

Lake-effect snow over the Great Lakes.

6

Number of states that have never had a blizzard

- The Great Plains area between Colorado and Minnesota is called Blizzard Alley.
- The Great Lakes region can have blizzards due to lake-effect snow. Cold Arctic air rushes over air warmed by the lakes.
- Once rare, blizzards are now happening more often.

Nor'easters

Satellite image of a nor'easter, 2018.

Combine a tornado with a blizzard. Add a flood and rain. Toss in ice, winds, and rough seas. What do you get? A nor'easter.

Nor'easters are extreme storms that develop along the East Coast. They strike New England and the Mid-Atlantic states.

Nor'easters form in the Atlantic about 100 miles (160 km) from shore. The polar jet stream brings cold air down to the warm ocean. When the different temperatures slam together, a severe storm results.

Not all nor'easters are big storms. Many are destructive. Most nor'easters develop in the

fall and winter. They bring lots of cold air and rainfall to the coastal areas. Heavy snow and winds can lead to a blizzard.

The Atlantic coast of the US has many large cities such as Boston, New York City, and Washington, DC. This means that one storm can affect millions of people.

THINK ABOUT IT

There are up to 40 nor'easters in a year. How would you decide if special preparations are needed?

1,200
Diameter in miles (1,900 km) of some nor'easters

- Nor'easters are named for the direction from which the strong winds blow, the northeast.
- Nor'easters get power from cold air, while hurricanes strengthen in warm air.
- Over 100 million people were affected by a 2016 nor'easter.

Blizzards can make driving hard.

11

People Who Watch for Blizzards

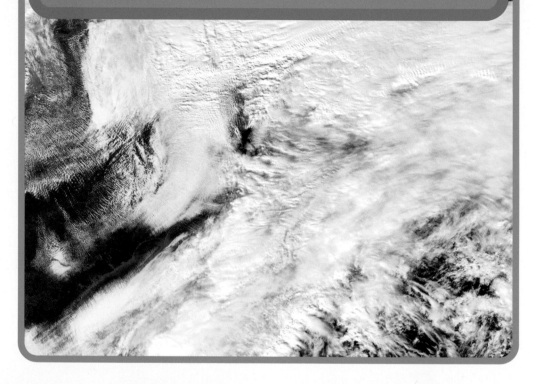

Blizzards develop over several days. This time allows scientists called meteorologists to predict them before they happen. Meteorologists can warn the public. Then people can prepare.

Computer models are used to predict the

An anemometer.

weather. A model is a set of math equations. It uses past weather data and patterns to guess the future. Current and old data are entered into a supercomputer to make a forecast.

The National Weather Service (NWS) collects data used for the models. The data come from many sources. Radar tracks precipitation. Anemometers measure wind speed. Satellites track weather patterns from space. The NWS meteorologists use several models when they make a forecast. The models use the information different ways.

16,500

Speed in miles per hour (26,500 km/h) at which polar satellites travel

- Polar satellites orbit the Earth from pole to pole 14 times daily.
- The NWS gives their data to the public. Private companies can use the data to make their own forecasts.
- Weather balloons are used to collect data high in the atmosphere.

HOW ACCURATE ARE THE PREDICTIONS?

Five-day weather forecasts are correct 90 percent of the time. However, predicting blizzards can be tricky. The weather patterns that trigger blizzards also trigger other storms.

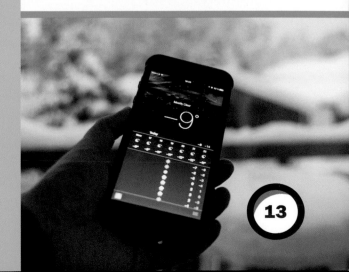

13

Ready for the Weather?

A meteorologist studying weather patterns.

The news issues a winter weather warning. Should people worry?

The National Weather Service (NWS) provides weather alerts. These alerts help keep people safe in severe storms. The NWS employs meteorologists, scientists who predict the weather. The NWS sends alerts to governments and television stations. These groups share the forecasts with the public.

The NWS provides alerts about many kinds of winter weather.

They warn for blizzards, winter storms, or extreme cold. An *advisory* tells people to be aware that extreme weather may be coming. A *watch* says to prepare for winter weather soon. A *warning* means take action now to be safe.

The rules for an alert depend on location. A winter storm warning in Alabama will be based on far less snow than a warning in the snowy Dakotas.

Cities and states prepare when they are told that blizzard weather is coming. They may close schools. They may warn people not to travel.

50,000
Approximate number of warnings issued by the NWS each year

- Blizzard warnings are issued when blizzard conditions are expected within 12 to 24 hours.
- Members of the public use email, texts, websites, apps, radio, or TV to get alerts.
- A winter weather advisory may warn of snow, sleet, freezing rain, or blowing snow.

Blizzards can cause extreme snowfall.

Digging Out After a Blizzard

A snow melter.

The blizzard is over. What happens now? It is hard work cleaning up after one of those storms. Cities plow the roads. When the piles of snow at the sides of the roads get too big, the snow is hauled away. Some cities load the snow in trucks and dump it in fields. Some cities use snow melters.

Workers repair downed power lines. Other crews remove trees and branches. They tow stranded cars.

Sometimes people are trapped in their cars. First responders go out to the streets and highways. They help lost and stranded people.

An adult should check for fallen power lines before anyone goes out. They should also check the roof, windows, and water pipes. Everyone can help clear the snow. Then, if school is still canceled, everyone can have a great time playing outside.

THINK ABOUT IT

How could you help neighbors after a blizzard?

350

Amount of snow in tons (300 metric tons) that a snow melter can process in one hour

- In 1992, Syracuse, New York, banned all snow. The joke law could not protect America's snowiest major city.
- The first blizzard declared a federal disaster area was in 1977 in New York State. Some drifts were as high as telephone poles.
- North Dakota holds the record for most snow angels (8,962) made in one place at the same time.

A Very Snowy Decade

Laura Ingalls Wilder and her little house.

Severe blizzards haunted the 1880s. A series of storms occurred from 1880 to 1881 in the Dakota Territory. The writer Laura Ingalls Wilder made these blizzards famous. The snow was so deep that no supplies reached her town for many months.

Between 1885 and 1888, there were many dreadful blizzards. A volcanic eruption in the South Pacific may have helped cause them. The volcano spewed ash and gas into the atmosphere. This lowered temperatures around the world for several years.

The Great Blizzard, 1888.

In 1887, a summer drought reduced grassy pastures in Wyoming, Montana, and the Dakotas. The ranchers did not store feed for the cattle. Then a severe blizzard covered the grass. Millions of cattle starved to death.

Finally, in 1888, a blizzard hit the New England area. Snow fell unexpectedly. People caught outside sheltered in prisons and hotels. About 15,000 were stranded in trains. This problem led to the development of the subway.

90

Percent of cattle that were killed in the blizzards of 1887

- After the 1888 blizzard, companies began to bury power lines.
- Some drifts in New York City reached the second floor.
- Rainy Seattle received over five feet (1.5 m) of snow in January 1880.

The Storm of the Century

Blizzards can cause roads to close.

No one expects a blizzard when the temperature is 80°F (27°C). Even so, that is what happened in Georgia in 1993. On a warm, sunny March day, the storm of the century slammed the state.

How? First, a powerful storm formed in the Gulf of Mexico. It slung thunderstorms and tornadoes across Florida. The storm stretched to Cuba and headed north. Massive snow and blizzard conditions hit many states, including Georgia.

Digging out after the *snowicane*.

40

Percent of the population in the US affected by the 1993 superstorm

- Because winds reached hurricane speeds, some people called the storm a *snowicane*.
- Nearly 10 million people on the eastern seaboard lost power.
- The storm caused $5.5 billion in damages.

Nearly 3 feet (1 m) of snow fell. Snow even fell in parts of Florida.

By the time the storm ended, it had reached Maine and Canada. Schools, highways, airports, and businesses closed.

Dozens of sailors and fishers were lost at sea. Waves reached 65 feet (20 m) high. The storm took about 300 lives.

DATA FARMING

Before radar and satellites, scientists gathered weather data from farmers and sailors. They were the best weather watchers. In 1920, Lewis Fry Richardson attempted the first mathematical weather forecast. He spent 6 weeks crunching numbers.

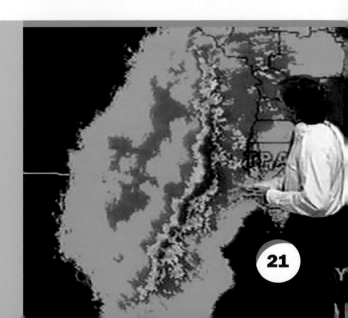

Climate Change and Changing Weather Patterns

Rising temperatures on Earth are making weather more extreme. Climate change happens when weather patterns shift over a long period of time. The current change is partly due to human activities and habits. Rising temperatures bring surprising changes.

First, the oceans warm. They evaporate more moisture in the air above the water. Storms soak up this extra moist air. Then they carry it over the land. The extra

Snowplows clearing heavy snow.

22

Warmer temperatures lead to worse blizzards.

moisture falls in the form of rain and snow.

A second factor is Arctic warming. Melting sea ice leads to a warmer Arctic. Warm temperatures there alter the jet stream. The jet stream is a powerful ribbon of wind in Earth's atmosphere. If the windy ribbon bends, it swings south. More cold air spills over warm oceans. These conditions can cause more storms, including blizzards.

These changes are seen beyond the US. Europe now has worse blizzards. And further south, heavy rainfall and storms are causing disasters in Asia.

455 billion

Approximate tons (413 billion metric tons) of polar ice lost each year

- Polar bears cannot trek across melting sea ice to hunt.
- Sea level has risen 8 inches (20 cm) since 1880.
- A winter storm in February 2021 cause power outages for 9.9 million people in the Southern US and Mexico.

THINK ABOUT IT

How might changing patterns affect the weather where you live?

Blizzards Around the World

Afghanistan blizzard, 2008.

Besides the US, blizzards are common in China and Russia. The deadliest blizzard in history occurred in Iran. Normally, this country is dry and hot. It receives little rainfall in a year. A blizzard was a big surprise. About 26 feet (8 m) of snow fell in a 1972 storm. The snow covered 200 villages. Over 4,000 people died.

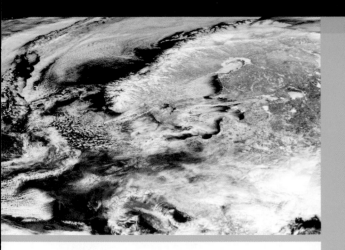

13 trillion

Amount of water in tons (12 trillion metric tons) stored in all the clouds around the planet

- The Iran blizzard happened after a four-year drought.
- Hundreds of thousands of animals died in the Afghan blizzard.
- In 2018, a major storm was called the "Beast from the East." The blizzard swept into Europe from Siberia.

In 2008, another deadly blizzard slammed Afghanistan. That country is next to Iran. Temperatures sank. Heavy snow fell. Once again, the blizzard surprised people. The storm claimed over 900 lives.

BLIZZARDS IN THE TROPICS

It is possible to have a blizzard in the tropics. If people go high up a mountain, like Mount Kilimanjaro in Africa, they will reach areas that are like the Arctic. They may experience a blizzard.

Mount Kilimanjaro.

The Cold Antarctic

Icebergs in Antarctica.

Snow drifts and snow plains reach to the horizon. Wind gusts so fast it feels like a solid wall. Snowflakes and pellets swirl wildly. Welcome to Antarctica.

Antarctica is larger than the United States and Mexico combined. It is covered with huge sheets of ice and snow. Oddly, blizzards almost never occur there. Why? Antarctica is actually a desert. Very little new snow falls there each year.

However, ground blizzards are common. Winds can be higher than 60 miles per hour (100 km/h) for days and days. Gusts can

-144°

Lowest Earth temperature in degrees Fahrenheit (−98°C) ever recorded by satellite

- Temperatures in the Antarctic are usually below zero all year.
- Antarctica's unique winds are called *katabatics*. They form as air rushes down slopes.
- Antarctica is warming faster than anywhere else on Earth.

reach 200 miles per hour (320 km/h)—faster than a hurricane.

The scientists who work in Antarctica leave in the winter.

The cold is too harsh. Penguins stay year-round. When blizzards rage, penguin colonies huddle together. The penguins on the outside gradually shuffle to the center to warm up.

The memorial to Robert Falcon Scott and his team.

A DOOMED EXPEDITION

In 1912, a British expedition led by Robert Falcon Scott reached the South Pole. On their way home, they were caught in a severe blizzard. They died from starvation and cold.

27

Staying Safe in a Blizzard

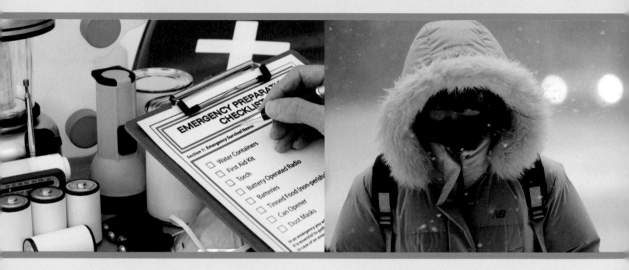

- Have a three-day supply of food and water, flashlights, and medications in an emergency kit.

- Stay off the roads.

- If you are trapped in a vehicle during a blizzard, don't leave the car.

- Stay indoors as much as you can.

- If you have to go outside, dress warmly. Protect your face.

- Bring pets inside and make sure large animals, such as horses, have shelter.

- Have lots of blankets and coats in case the power goes out.

- Have a shovel in the house in case you have to dig yourself out.

Glossary

alert
A notification of a possible danger or problem.

atmosphere
The layer or layers of gases surrounding a planet.

drought
A long period of dry weather with little or no rainfall, often over months or years

federal disaster area
An area that gets help from the federal government after heavy damage by natural hazards.

frostbite
The severe damage caused when extreme cold temperatures freeze fingers, toes, or other exposed skin.

hypothermia
The dangerous condition where a person's temperature drops well below 95°F (35°C).

jet stream
A band of powerful winds high in the atmosphere that blow from west to east. They push and separate hot and cold air masses.

meteorologist
A scientist who studies and predicts the weather.

precipitation
Water particles that fall from the sky in the form of rain, snow, sleet, or hail.

weather balloon
A balloon equipped with tools that is sent into the atmosphere to gather information about the weather.

whiteout
A weather condition in which blowing snow makes it almost impossible to see.

windchill
The measurement of how cold it feels from a combination of the air temperature and the wind speed.

Read More

Cosgrove, Brian. *Weather: Discover the World's Weather from Heat Waves and Droughts to Blizzards and Flood.* New York: DK Children, 2016.

Keppeler, Jill. *Blasted by Blizzards.* New York: Rosen PowerKids Press, 2018.

Meister, Cari. *Blizzards.* Minneapolis, MN: Jump! 2016.

Visit 12StoryLibrary.com

Scan the code or use your school's login at **12StoryLibrary.com** for recent updates about this topic and a full digital version of this book. Enjoy free access to:

- Digital ebook
- Breaking news updates
- Live content feeds
- Videos, interactive maps, and graphics
- Additional web resources

Note to educators: Visit 12StoryLibrary.com/register to sign up for free premium website access. Enjoy live content plus a full digital version of every 12-Story Library book you own for every student at your school.

Index

About the Author

Liam Corrigan is fascinated by physics, the weather, and artificial intelligence. He also enjoys listening to podcasts, practicing yoga, and traveling.

READ MORE FROM 12-STORY LIBRARY

Every 12-Story Library Book is available in many formats. For more information, visit **12StoryLibrary.com**